# HOW

## Many arms does a star fish have?

Om KIDZ

An imprint of Om Books International

# Contents

## How big is the ocean?

It covers approximately 71% of the Earth's surface! An ocean is a continuous body of salt water contained in huge basins on the Earth's surface. It is often divided into five large ocean basins that cover around 360,000,000 km$^2$ (almost 71%) of the Earth's surface and hold over 1.3 billion km$^3$ of water.

**Find out**

What do we call scientists who study the ocean?

**Pocket fact**

**We are unique!**
Earth is the only known planet to have large bodies of liquid water on its surface. Our planet is neither too hot nor too cold and has appropriate atmospheric pressure. This prevents liquid surface water from evaporating into space.

### How many oceans are there in the world?

There are five oceans in the world that are separated by large areas of land called continents. These are the Atlantic Ocean, Pacific Ocean, Indian Ocean, Arctic Ocean and Southern Ocean. The Atlantic, Pacific and Indian Oceans are linked in the south by the Southern Ocean whereas the Arctic Ocean lies in the north.

## How do seas and oceans get their name?

Based on their location, features and more! The five oceans of the world are named on the basis of their different characteristics. The Indian Ocean is named so, simply because it lies to the south of India. The Pacific Ocean was named so based on its calmness. The Atlantic Ocean was named after Atlas, the Titan of Greek mythology, who supported the heavens with his great strength. The Arctic Ocean got its name from the Greek word arktos, meaning 'bear' and the Antarctic simply means 'opposite to the Arctic'.

### Pocket fact

**Gold in the water!**

Gold is not only found deep inside the Earth but also in the ocean. It is estimated that the world's oceans contain about twenty million tons of gold.

### Find out

Are there flower-bearing plants under the ocean?

## How did the Red Sea get its name?

It's because of certain algae! The Red Sea is situated between Asia and Africa; it is usually blue-green in colour. The Red Sea got its name from the colour changes observed in its water. It is populated by large blooms of the algae *Trichodesmium erythraeum*, which turn the sea reddish-brown in colour upon dying off.

## How much salt do seas and oceans have?

The concentration of salt in seawater is called salinity. The range of salinity observed in the ocean is almost 33–37 grams of salt per litre of seawater. This means that every 1 litre (1000 ml) of seawater has 33–37 grams of salt dissolved in it.

**Pocket fact**

**Antifreeze!**
Some animals in the Antarctic have natural antifreeze in their blood to prevent freezing.

**Find out**

Why has the Black Sea been named so?

## How do plants and animals survive in salt water?

Different creatures have different adaptations! The concentration of salt in seawater is very high. Fish survive in seas and oceans by eliminating the salt, they take in with water, through their gills. They also use their kidneys and ion pumps to excrete the extra salt. Crocodiles living in seawater have special glands in their tongues that help them eliminate salt. On the other hand, many ocean plants adapt to the salinity by breaking down the salt into chlorine and sodium ions.

## How can plants grow in the ocean without the sun?

They do receive sunlight to a certain depth! Sunlight can penetrate the ocean to a depth called the euphotic zone or sunlight zone. About 90% of plants and animals that live in the ocean are present in this zone. Plants like seaweed or kelp can grow here in the presence of sunlight.

### Pocket fact

**I am faster underwater!**
Sound travels faster underwater than in the air. The speed of sound underwater is 1434 metres per second, which is almost 4.3 times faster than the speed of sound in the air.

### Find out

What is the temperature of underwater hot springs?

## How do marine mammals stay warm?

The blubber helps them keep warm! Mammals are warm-blooded, that is their body temperature does not change according to the temperature outside. So they need to adjust to the changing temperatures. Marine mammals have a thick layer of fat tissue called blubber, which is made of adipose tissue. This tissue does not transfer heat easily and helps to insulate the mammal's body.

## How deep do submarines dive?

Up to a depth of 14,760 feet! A submarine is a watercraft that can operate underwater at very high pressure. Submarines are built with special sealed compartments that open up and fill with water. This weighs the boat down so that it sinks. As of 2023, the deepest a submarine has gone is 35,849 feet underwater.

### Pocket fact

**Dive in!**
The first expedition to take samples from the hadal zone was the trail-blazing HMS Challenger Expedition. It worked from 1872 to 1876. Scientists managed to extract samples from 26,246 feet under the ocean.

### Find out

Do submarines operate on the echolocation technique?

## How far can sunlight penetrate into the ocean?

Not beyond 200 metres (656 feet)! The ocean is divided into three main zones based on depth and the light that reaches it. Sunlight can penetrate up to 200 metres inside the ocean. This upper 200 metres of the ocean is called the euphotic or sunlight zone. It is home to many marine mammals and sea turtles. Only a small amount of light penetrates beyond this zone, which is the twilight zone.

## How are chimneys made under the sea?

When seawater circulates through hot volcanic rocks! Many times seawater circulates through hot volcanic rocks and comes in contact with molten magma. It then gets heated and rises back to the surface through the fissures. This extremely hot seawater then gushes out of the holes in the crust and mixes with the cold seawater. The minerals suspended in the hot water clump together and drop out at the vent opening. This leads to the formation of structures called chimneys.

**Find out**

Visit a library and look at the pictures of rocks and stones that are found under the ocean. Name a few of them.

**Pocket fact**

**Underwater lakes!**
You can find not only volcanoes and mountains but also lakes and rivers under the ocean. These lakes are called brine pools and have their own shorelines.

## How old is the ocean floor?

Over 4 billion years old! Earlier, the age of the oldest oceanic rocks was determined to be approximately 200 million years. But in 2008, geologists found that the formation of the oceanic rock dates back to almost 4.28 billion years ago. The crust on the Nuvvuagittuq Greenstone Belt, on the eastern shore of Hudson Bay, is said to have formed when the Earth was still cooling from its formation!

## How are tides predicted?

Predictions and real-time observations of tides are based on many factors! Occurrence of tides is based on the movements of the Sun, the moon and the Earth. Scientists use advanced tidal recording systems and study images sent by satellites to monitor tides and water levels. These data are used to predict ocean behaviour in order to protect our coasts and coastal communities. Most coastal areas experience two low tides and two high tides every 24 hours and 50 minutes.

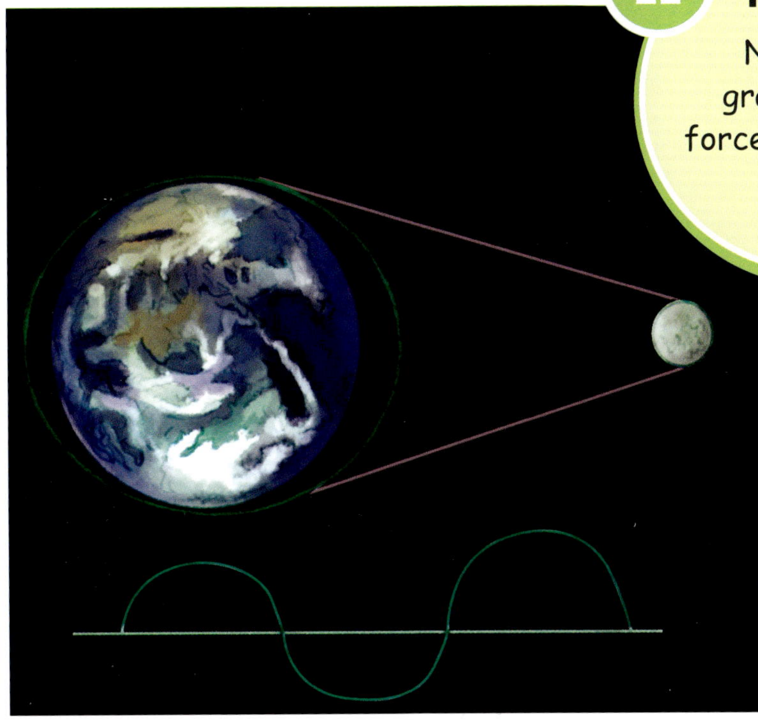

**Find out**

Name the gravitational force that causes tides.

**Pocket fact**

**Neap is weak!**
When the moon is in its first and last quarter phase there is interference between the sun and the moon's gravitational pull. This results in weaker tidal troughs called Neap Tides.

## How are tides helpful to us?

Tides are useful to us in many ways! Tidal energy is harnessed to produce electricity. Dams built along water bodies get filled up during high tide and this water is used to produce hydroelectricity. Tides are a great help in navigation. During high tide when the water level rises, large ships can enter or leave the harbour safely.

## How are coral reefs formed?

They are built by colonies of tiny animals found in marine water. A coral reef is a ridge or hummock formed in the shallow ocean area by algae and stony corals. The stony corals are made up of tiny, soft colonial organisms called polyps. As the polyps die they leave their skeletons behind. Layers of these skeletons are covered by living polyps eventually forming coral reefs.

**Pocket fact**

**Algae tonic!**
Different types of microscopic algae called Symbiodinium live inside the cells of the coral. They provide the coral with food and help them grow faster.

**Find out**

Where do the starfish get their nutrition from?

## How many arms does a starfish have?

They have five arms! Starfish are marine invertebrates. Their body is made up of a central disc, grooves with rows of tube feet and usually five arms. Their arms are hollow and covered with short spines and pincer-like organs called pedicellariae. A starfish can lose one or more arms and grow new ones!

## How did sea anemones get their name?

It is named after a flower! Sea anemones are soft-bodied marine animals that resemble flowers. Their body is cylindrical in shape with an oral disk that contains the mouth. The upper end of the body is surrounded by petal-like tentacles which are often present in multiples of six. These beautiful creatures get their name from the terrestrial anemone flower that is similar in appearance to the sea anemone.

**Find out**

Which land mammal uses echolocation to know its surroundings better?

**Pocket fact**

**That's big!**

A sea anemone can have a diameter of up to 1.8–3 cm. One of the largest sea anemones found had a diameter of 6.6 feet.

## How do dolphins use sound to see?

By the process of echolocation! Dolphins and some other marine mammals locate objects with the help of echolocation. Dolphins produce high-frequency sounds that travel through the water around them. These sound waves bounce back from the creatures and objects in the water, thus allowing the dolphins to sense their surroundings.

## How are sand dollars well-adapted for burrowing in the sand?

They have spines for digging! Sand dollars are marine animals with a flat, disk-shaped body. Their mouth is located at the centre of the body's underside. Its upper surface exhibits symmetry with a pattern of five 'petals' spreading out from the centre. It has very small spines on the entire surface of its body. These spines are appressed backwards towards the posterior anus and help it in digging and crawling.

### Pocket fact

**Just count the rings!**
You can determine the age of a sand dollar specimen by simply counting the rings on its exoskeleton. Sand dollars usually live for 6–10 years!

### Find out

Collect some seashells and observe the patterns on them. Do you find any similarity in the patterns?

## How are seashells formed?

Seashells are the hard outer skeletons of marine molluscs, such as snails, that protect their bodies. As molluscs grow, they take in salts and chemicals from the water around them. As they process these materials they secrete calcium carbonate, which hardens on the outside of their bodies. This eventually forms a hard outer shell. When these molluscs die they leave their shells behind, for us to find, along the sea shore.

## How does an octopus hide itself?

It has a unique way of camouflaging! An octopus can contract its muscles to change both colour and shape. It has special skin cells called chromatophores that are full of yellow, red, brown and black pigments. This can help it change colour to blend in with its surroundings so as to avoid predators.

### Pocket fact

**We are ovoviviparous!**
Sawfish are ovoviviparous, that is their young ones are hatched from eggs; however, these eggs hatch inside the mother's body. The young ones are nourished by a yolk sac.

### Find out

How many hearts does an octopus have?

## How does a sawfish use its saw?

Sawfish are found in shallow water in the tropical and subtropical regions of the world. They have a long snout called 'rostrum' edged with sharp teeth and thousands of tiny sensors. These sensors can detect invisible electric fields that surround living organisms. Using these special sensors, sawfish can locate fish swimming in the waters around them. Then they use their rostrum to catch and kill their prey.

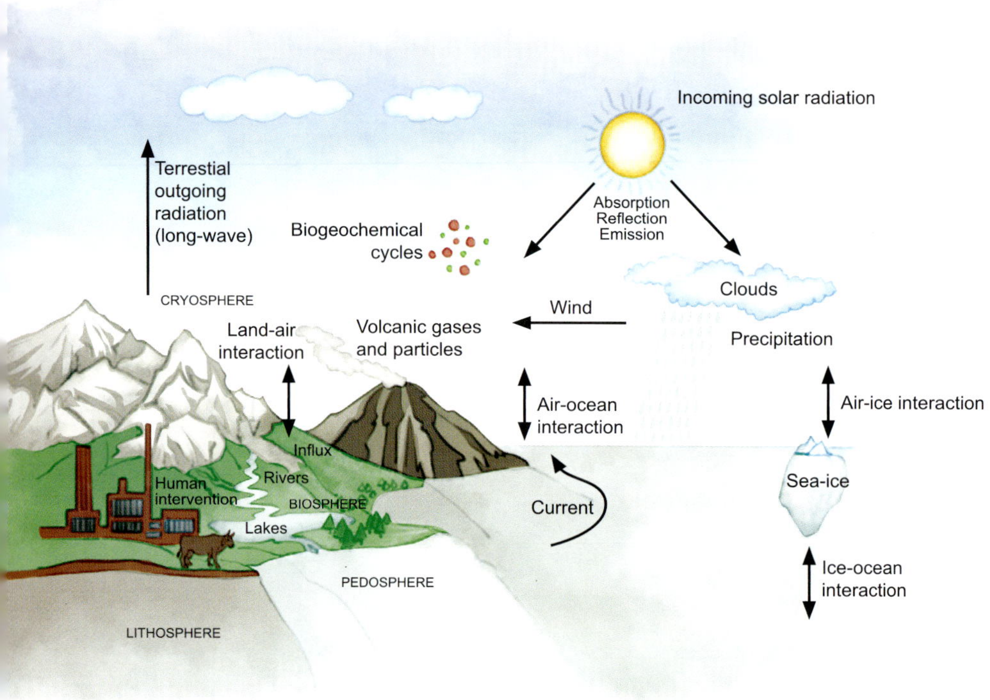


## How do oceans affect the Earth's climate?

They act as huge solar panels! Sun is the major source of heat and light on Earth. While land and atmosphere absorb some sunlight, the majority of the sun's radiation is absorbed by the ocean, particularly by the tropical waters around the equator. The ocean stores the radiation from the Sun and distributes it globally with the help of winds and ocean currents.

### Pocket fact

**It's not amazing!**
The North Pacific Gyre is an ocean garbage site off the coast of California. It is twice as large as the state of Texas and is the largest ocean garbage site in the world.

### Find out

Why is the sea warmer at night?

## How does the ocean get polluted?

When harmful substances are disposed in the ocean! Ocean pollution is caused when harmful substances, such as oil, plastic, chemicals and agricultural waste are disposed into the ocean. Large-scale oil spills also pollute the ocean. In many parts of the world, people dump trash directly into the ocean. This litters the ocean with waste which is harmful to plants and animals.

## How does ocean pollution affect marine life?

It causes a lot of harm! Ocean pollution severely affects marine life. The chemicals disposed in the ocean accumulate in the tissues of marine animals and cause organ malfunctions. Plastic waste is often mistaken for food by marine animals and it kills them when they eat it. Oil from oil spills destroys the insulating ability of fur-bearing mammals and exposes them to harsh elements, thus killing them.

### Pocket fact

**The cleanest!**
Antarctica is the cleanest place on Earth. The continent is protected by strong anti-pollution laws.

### Find out

How can we prevent the pollution of water bodies on Earth? Discuss with your parents.

## How can we help in keeping the ocean clean?

By proper waste disposal! It is essential to throw trash in the correct waste bin to prevent pollution. We can help clean up the garbage in rivers, lakes and on the beaches. We should not throw litter down the drain. We should use eco-friendly cleaning liquids. It is also important to ensure the proper disposal of toxic household chemicals.

# Index